BMX Billy

Billy had a BMX bike

but he had nowhere to ride it.

4

The yard was too small.
The park was too neat.
The street was too busy.
"Where can I ride
my bike?" he said.

One day, Billy's father

took him to a BMX dirt track.

"Whoop-de-do!"
yelled Billy,
and ZOOM,
away he went
down the track.

8

Billy went *THUMP* over the bumps, and *SPLASH* through the mud.

11

He jumped over humps and tried tricky stunts. Sometimes they worked, and sometimes they didn't.

But Billy and his BMX friends

had lots of fun!